Walter Trobisch

Love is a Feeling to be Learned

other books by the Trobisches:
A Baby Just Now?
Better Is Your Love Than Wine
I Loved a Girl
I Married You
The Joy of Being a Woman
Living with Unfulfilled Desires
Love Yourself
My Beautiful Feeling
On Our Way Rejoicing

booklets by Walter Trobisch:
Martin Luther's Quiet Time
Spiritual Dryness

WALTER TROBISCH

LOVE
is a Feeling
to be
Learned

INTER-VARSITY PRESS
Downers Grove, Illinois 60515

© 1971 by Editions Trobisch, D-757 Baden-Baden (Germany)

Published in America by InterVarsity Press with permission from Editions Trobisch.

InterVarsity Press is the book-publishing division of Inter-Varsity Christian Fellowship, a student movement active on campus at hundreds of universities, colleges and schools of nursing. For information about local and regional activities, write IVCF, 233 Langdon St., Madison, WI 53703.

Distributed in Canada through InterVarsity Press, 1875 Leslie St., Unit 10, Don Mills, Ontario M3B 2M5, Canada.

ISBN 0-87784-314-7

Printed in the United States of America

21	20	19	18	17	16	15	14	13	12	11	10	9
92	91	90	89	88	87	86	85	84	83	82	81	80

In India, one tells this legend about the creation of man and woman:

When he had finished creating the man, the Creator realized that he had used up all the concrete elements. There was nothing solid, nothing compact or hard, left over to create the woman.

After thinking for a long time, the Creator took

the roundness of the moon, the flexibility of a clinging vine and the trembling of grass,

the slenderness of a reed and the blossoming of flowers,

the lightness of leaves and the serenity of the rays of sunshine,

the tears of clouds and the instability of the wind,

the fearfulness of a rabbit and the vanity of a peacock,

the softness of a bird's breast and the hardness of a diamond, the sweetness of honey and the cruelty of a tiger,

the burning of fire and the coldness of snow,

the talkativeness of a magpie and the singing of a nightingale,

the falseness of a crane and the faithfulness of a mother lion.

Mixing all these non-solid elements together, the Creator created the woman and gave her to the man.

After one week, the man came back and said:

"Lord, the creature that you have given to me makes my life unhappy. She talks without ceasing and torments me intolerably, so that I have no rest. She insists that I pay attention to her all the time and so my hours are wasted. She cries about every little thing and leads an idle life. I have come to give her back to you, because I can't live with her."

The Creator said: "All right." And he took her back.

After a week had passed, the man came back to the Creator and said: "Lord, my life is so empty since I gave that creature back to you. I always think of her — how she danced and sang, how she looked at me out of the corner of her eye, how she chatted with me and then snuggled close to me. She was so beautiful to look at and so soft to touch. I liked so much to hear her laugh. Please give her back to me."

The Creator said: "All right." And he gave her back.

But three days later, the man came back again and said:

"Lord, I don't know — I just can't explain it, but after all my experience with this creature, I've come to the conclusion that she causes me more trouble than pleasure. I pray thee, take her back again! I can't live with her!"

The Creator replied: "You can't live without her either!"

And he turned his back to the man and continued his work.

The man said in desperation: "What shall I do? I can't live *with* her and I can't live *without* her!"

L ove is a feeling to be learned.

It is tension and fulfillment.

It is deep longing and hostility.

It is gladness and it is pain.

There is not one without the other.

Happiness is only a part of love — this is what has to be learned. Suffering belongs to love also. This is the mystery of love, its beauty and its burden.

Love is a feeling to be learned.

It caused Sylvia almost physical pain to give up her dream. But now she was sure: This was the end of it.

Before she had met him, she had had a dream image of what her future husband would be like: tall, slim, a good athlete, intelligent, full of spirit, a university graduate, a few years older than she, and, of course, a lover of music and poetry, possibly a professor of English literature or religion or a holder of a well-paid job with the government.

When she passed a florist shop and saw the dark-red roses in the window, Sylvia pictured to herself just how it would be some day when someone would bring her such roses as a declaration of his love.

Gone was the dream! He was so different. There was absolutely nothing exciting about him. When he had asked her for their first date she had prayed in her heart: "Please, Lord, not him! He's not the one I want to marry!"

She had never been interested in technical things and that was his whole field of interest, because he was a construction engineer. He also was rather dull. No, he didn't bring her roses. He didn't bring her anything. He just came and there he was.

He was so down to earth and so sober.

Not that he was without feeling. But just the expression of his feelings irritated her. She couldn't rely upon them, because they could change so quickly. One minute he was impetuous and enthusiastic and the next he was as solemn as a stick. When she longed for a tender word, he offered her a kiss instead, and in the same breath talked about football or his studies.

Everything was reason and will with him. He called her stupid and sentimental when she put more faith in her intuition than in his reasoning and thinking.

Why can't a boy be like a girl?

Sometimes she wanted to be like a porcupine, roll together and show her prickles in order to make him understand in a thorny way that moonlight did not increase her desire for contact.

In his presence, she felt the desire to withdraw into the fortress of freedom and hoist the flag of independence.

Yet Sylvia did not send him away. Not yet, she thought; maybe later on.

But later on, a half a year or so, a few things dawned on her. She began to understand that a young man who sends a book to her which interests him, may be more serious than someone who sends roses.

The book says: I want to share something with you which moves my heart at present. I want to give you a part in my life. I want to know what you think. It is important to me to know what you think.

She discovered to her astonishment one day, that she had stopped to look at a bridge. For the first time she saw the beauty of its swing, of its lines. Or she stood and watched as the beams for a skyscraper were hoisted upwards and thought: I should show this to him.

It was no longer important to her just to be understood. She herself had begun to understand. She had learned the first lesson in love: one has to give up dreams, because they stand in the way of happiness.

Love is a special way of feeling — something to be learned.

I f this special way of feeling is not learned, if there is no romance in the relationship between the sexes, sex and love become the same thing. This is still true to a great extent in Africa. Sex is called love and love is called sex. "I loved a girl" means "I went to bed with a girl". If this special feeling is not learned, there is either nothing or everything. There is no in-between.

The consequences of this attitude are tremendous. The woman becomes little more than a womb, a well-equipped incubator. She is not a person, but a thing which can be traded, bought and sold, given and taken, exchanged and disposed of, an inferior being without a will of her own, obedient to masculine wishes. In any culture where there is little sexual restraint, no romance and no in-between, the result is that the girl becomes simply a thing, a matter, an object.

What Africa needs more than anything else is to learn how to love.

But, can we say that it has been learned in Western culture? What do African students experience when they come to Europe or America?

Do they find anything different here from what they have left at home? The so-called "New Morality", the much-called-for sexual liberty in the West, did not emancipate the woman but degraded her, made her lose her dignity and personality. In Europe and America too, it made out of her a thing, a toy, a tool, an object to satisfy masculine wishes.

All of us have to learn how to love, to appreciate the beauty of the in-between, the joy of the preliminary.

Sylvia said: "There was an easiness in our relationship, the easiness of something not yet final, and that is what I appreciated the most. In this easiness there was at the same time greatness and depth. It was just this easiness, this lightness, which gave our friendship promise.

"The easiness of the in-between did not mean that there was no pain of longing and no suffering of suspense. But it bound pain and suffering together with deep-felt happiness."

Did you hear? Pain and suffering! The hit-songs and movies lie to us when they try to tell us that happiness can be had without suffering. Just here is the reason for the failure of many a relationship, for the frustrations and torture, yes, even for the shallowness and shipwreck of many a marriage: to think that love can grow and live without suffering.

Love and suffering do not exclude each other. Rather they condition each other.

Sex problems may have their deepest roots in the refusal to accept suffering, in wanting to jump over the in-between stage with its tension and anxiety, thus making the word "love" an empty word.

It pays to suffer lover's grief.

Suffering is not something to be eliminated, regardless of the cost. If we live through it and accept it, suffering can become a spring of riches, of depth, growth and fulfillment — yes, of happiness.

Therefore, I say, in contradiction to the popular songs of today: It pays to suffer lover's grief.

John sat and thought.

It had happened again. His girl friend had broken off with him.

He really couldn't understand why. True, he had made mistakes. Maybe he had even taken too much for granted — too much and too soon.

He had felt all the time that she had never taken their relationship as seriously as he did. Maybe she was afraid to do so.

Though they were both of the same age, he always felt so inferior to her, so unsure of himself in her presence. Sometimes he had the impression that she was years older, while he felt like a baby with a beard.

Why can't a man be like a woman?

Anyway, he had to accept her decision. It was painful and his heart ached, but he didn't want to drown out the pain or dance it to death. He wanted to take it seriously.

So he sat and thought.

Maybe this was the purpose of suffering — to teach him how to discern between the true and the false, and above all, to teach him the art of sacrifice.

It pays to suffer lover's grief, if sacrifice is learned. The art of giving up, of letting go, is the most important art to be learned.

Not just for love's sake. I personally believe that the survival of mankind depends upon whether or not we give up the consumers' attitude and learn the art of sacrificing, not only our dreams, but also our desires which could be realized and fulfilled.

Suffering makes immature love grow into mature love. Immature, unlearned love is egotistic love. It's the kind of love that a child has — a love which claims and wants and wants immediately. It cannot endure tension and has no patience with anything which stands in the way. It demands and consumes and tries to dominate.

As John sat and thought, the idea came to him that the greatest proof of his love to his girl friend was to give her the freedom to say "no". Mature love does not try to lord it over the other one, but it lets go. It sets free.

Suffering transformed John's love to a new dimension.

It pays to suffer lover's grief, for nothing prepares us better for marriage. Marital love is love which has learned to surrender and to renounce.

In marriage, one no longer says "yours", or "mine", but "ours".

This word "our" is always connected with sacrifice, with giving up:

giving up one's partner as he goes to work;

giving up free time and independent planning in the interest of the family;

giving up things which one could have afforded while working as a single person;

sacrificing for the sake of the children;

and perhaps the hardest sacrifice of all, giving up the children themselves when they start to go their own ways.

Maybe this is the root of the generation problem. Parents who have not learned the sacrificing art of love are unable to apply it now to their own children. They are like hens who hatch out duck's eggs and then stand at the edge of the pond and cackle and squawk while the young ducklings swim away.

They are still learning and their children have to be patient with them. Mark Twain once said: "When I was sixteen, I thought my dad was hopeless. When I was twenty, I was surprised to discover that he had made progress."

However, it can be true the other way too. Sometimes a "no" from our parents comes out of deep concern to teach us sacrificing love. By obeying this parental "no", a child may learn the art of giving up which will later on be the greatest help when he has to face the reality of love, shape his own marriage, and educate his own children.

The art of giving up, of renouncing, is also the secret of happiness in a single person's life. To give up one's self is as important for a single person as it is for one who is married.

Those who learn this art will never be lonesome, even if they are single. Those who don't, will always be lonesome, even though they are married.

The task we have to face is the same, whether we are married or single: *To live a fulfilled life in spite of many unfulfilled desires.*

Love is a feeling to be learned by the single person as well. Those who do not marry do not have to give up love, but they have to learn love which gives up — just as those who are married must learn it. One could even say that the desire to be married is the condition for a happy single life.

Though the task we have to face is the same, whether we are married or single, let us not make the mistake of thinking that our present state is permanent. Let us not burden our hearts with the fear of finality.

Marriage can be a task for a limited time and then it suddenly ends with the death of one partner. Being single can also be but a passing task.

God does not like the decisions for a life-time which we make out of resignation and disappointment. He wants us to live our life this day and to discover all the joyous possibilities of it with confidence and courage.

Evelyn sat in the bus and shut her eyes so that the other passengers would think she was asleep. But her heart sang with the rhythm of the wheels: "He loves me. I shall be his wife. He shall be my husband."

No, she would never be able to understand it. She couldn't even explain it — either to her mother or to her girl friend. She had known it in her heart from the moment they looked at each other and their eyes spoke: "I do mean you, and you alone, and you for my whole life."

How did Carl succeed? Had he outwitted her by pretending at first not to be interested? Had he been more clever than others in his methods?

No, he hadn't even had a method. His principle had not been: take the little finger carefully first and then the whole hand will follow by itself.

It was a rather insignificant event which made her understand for the first time his way of being a friend. It was during her first year at college that he had asked her for their first date on a Saturday evening, although he knew that she usually went home for the weekend to see her family and friends. When she accepted his invitation to attend a theatre performance at his school with him, he thanked her expressly for giving up her trip home.

It was through this gesture on his part that she understood for the first time — he does not just want to spend a pleasant evening, nor is he just looking for an enjoyable partner for a few hours, but with his invitation, he meant *her*.

Love is a feeling to be learned and Evelyn knew deep down in her heart that it can never be learned by sex. She would never have reached the certainty she now had. For like loud drums which drown out the leading melody of flutes, sex would have deafened her ears to the low and gentle overtones so essential for choice.

Carl would not have heard the singing of the nightingale, nor seen the trembling of grass, the flexibility of a clinging vine and the serenity of the rays of sunshine; nor would he have felt the instability of the wind and the softness of a bird's breast.

They would have missed the beauty of the in-between, the pain of waiting and the joy of suspense, the suffering which made them so happy.

Evelyn knew: Sex would have kept their love from a chance to grow. It would have meant picking the blossoms in April and therefore never harvesting the apples.

For love does not grow out of sex. Love must grow into sex. For Evelyn, love meant above all, confidence and trust, fellowship and common experience, shared hopes and sorrows. It called for a reliable and lasting relationship. For her, love was inseparable from permanence.

Could it be, Evelyn thought, while the bus was bringing her closer and closer to her friend — could it be that girls who allow premarital sex, or even seek it, have repressed their deepest feelings and longings? That they are not the ones who are especially passionate, but, on the contrary, are rather impassionate, calculating and even cold?

What is an old maid? Someone unable to love. Someone who represses his feelings and doesn't say yes to himself. There are teenage "old maids". There are also married "old maids". There are even male "old maids".

The opposite of the "old maid" is the virgin.

Virginity is not something negative, but something tremendously positive. It corresponds to the demands of the deepest nature of the girl. Virginity is preparedness for the fulness of love.

Sex may turn a girl into an old maid. Virginity turns her into a woman.

Carl felt that there was nothing which had helped his love for Evelyn to mature more than her virginity. Like a dam which helps to turn the power of water into electricity, restraint helps to turn the power of sex into love.

Two things in her virgin attitude had helped him — her attractiveness and her modesty. It is not enough to have one without the other.

Through her attractiveness she had taught him to love her so much that he was willing to pay a price, to make a sacrifice, for this love.

Through her modesty, she had directed his interest beyond her body to her soul and had helped him who was used to living in the realm of will and reason, to discover his own soul.

Maybe the girl has to be the teacher of the boy in this realm, Carl thought.

If she had been attractive without being modest, she would have directed him towards adventure, but not towards marriage.

Attractiveness alone, without modesty, would have tempted him to pay the lowest possible price to fulfill his desire.

If she had given in to his desire, she would have lost her attractiveness for him. Therefore, just because he loved her and did not want to lose her, he had secretly hoped for her resistance.

To refuse sex was a greater proof of her love than to grant it. By granting it she would have hurt their love.

Love can be hurt by sex. It can be killed by sex. Therefore, love has to be protected.

There is a verse in the Bible which has not yet received due attention in this respect. It is Genesis 2:25: "They were both naked, the man and the wife, and were not ashamed."

Naked and not ashamed.

"Naked" is not meant here in a physical sense only. It means to stand in front of each other stripped and undisguised, without pretention, without hiding anything, seeing the partner as he really is and showing myself to him as I really am — and still not to be ashamed.

Naked and not ashamed.

But this ultimate goal of mature love is promised only to those who, as the previous verse says, have left father and mother and cleave to each other, in other words, those who have been publicly and legally married.

These two — not the ones before or outside of marriage — become one flesh.

These two — not the ones before or outside of marriage — shall succeed in the tremendously difficult task: to face each other as they really are, to live with each other — naked and yet not ashamed.

Naked and not ashamed — this is what the Bible means by the word "to know". "Adam knew Eve, his wife."

To know in this way is not possible outside of marriage. If it is tried beforehand, love is hurt or even killed.

Therefore, love has not only to be learned; it has to be protected as well.

It has to be protected by divine will. By listening to human reason we cannot protect love.

The trend in Europe today is to question divine will in the name of love.

"Did God say?" they ask, like the serpent asked Eve in the Garden of Eden.

Is it not love, they ask, to shorten the torment of waiting by permitting premarital sex?

Is it not love, they ask, to train sex by encouraging masturbation and even homosexual relations among teen-agers?

Is it not love, they ask, to furnish high-schoolers with contraceptives?

Is it not love, they ask, to allow your marriage partner to have sex with someone else providing he is in love with that person?

Is it not love, they ask, to give the unmarried girl the right to have a baby?

I remember how, during the time of Hitler, a film was shown in Germany which told the story of a doctor whose wife had an incurable disease. In detail the film showed how she was tormented by her sickness until her husband killed her with an overdose of sedatives. When he was put on trial for murder, he defended himself by saying: "I loved my wife."

Here, God's commandment: "Thou shalt not kill" was questioned in the name of love.

The film was shown in 1940 and was used by Hitler as a psychological preparation for the killing of the incurable and insane, for exterminating life which he judged unworthy of living. The end was the assassination of six million Jews in the gas chambers of the concentration camps.

If we seek to set up the standards of love ourselves, we fall into the hands of the devil. When Germany questioned the commandment "Thou shalt not kill" in the name of love, she fell into the hands of the devil. When we question today the commandment "Thou shalt not commit adultery" in the name of love we fall equally into the hands of the devil.

Since we do not know what love is, love has to be protected by the One who is love Himself. There is never a contradiction between love and divine will. There is no action of love which goes against a commandment of God.

We always hurt our neighbor when we break a commandment, even if we don't see it immediately in our present situation. But God is greater than our situation. He looks beyond what I can see. He has the film of my whole life in view, and not just the snapshot of my present situation.

The life-view offers a different picture than the snapshot. Let me illustrate this by the case of François and Cecile, the young African couple whose correspondence with me is published in the book, "*I Loved a Girl*".[1]

Those who have read this book will know that François and Cecile saw no other way out in their position than to elope. Thus they consummated their marriage before they were legally married.

Who of us can judge them? Humanly we can understand why they acted as they did in such a difficult situation.

Still, if you would ask them today about their action, they would both say that they regret it. Although they are happily married now, they would say that, in the last analysis, the consummation of their marriage before the wedding hurt their love more than it helped it.

So it is that when we take a snapshot out of its

1. Harper and Row, New York — Lutterworth Press, London E. C. 4

context, it may often seem to our human understanding as if a pre- or extra-marital surrender, a beautiful lie, or a gentle murder is the way of love. But if the film of life gets into focus, the way always looks different.

If you examine a messed-up life, you will see that the mess always started with the transgression of a divine commandment.

Jesus says: "If you love me, you will keep my commandments."

We cannot love our neighbor, unless we love Jesus. We cannot love Jesus, unless we obey Him.

Only the one who really loves is able to obey.

Only the one who obeys is really able to love.

"And his commandments are not burdensome." (I John 5:3).

They are not a burden, but a help. They are not a load, but a force. They do not incapacitate us, but make us mature. Actually it is much simpler to keep them than to transgress them. Life becomes much more difficult and complicated if we try to discover ourselves what is good and bad.

I know that there are some people who claim that it is normal among teen-agers today to practice premarital sex. There are even some statistics published which give frighteningly high numbers. To this I would like to say: Let us be careful with statistics in this field. There is no foolproof method whatsoever to arrive at scientifically reliable results concerning intimate behavior.

But even if these statistics were right, even if a high percentage practice premarital sex? So what?

Since when are Christians led by statistics? Since when are we guided by what the majority does? "We are a peculiar people." (I Peter 2:9). Are we or are we not? Christians are not shy animals who have to accept a protective coloring in order to be able to survive. On the contrary, unless we show our colors, we will not survive.

Bonhoeffer says: "Only the extraordinary is essentially Christian."

To conclude, let me tell you about my conversation with Karin, as we shall call her.

As I talked with her, Karin assured me several times that she had been involved in deep petting with her boy friend, but that they had never gone "all the way".

I did not ask her any questions. But the next day, Karin came back. She wanted to know what is really meant by the expression: "going all the way".

I said, "Karin, I think what is meant is the complete physical union."

This answer did not satisfy her. She asked me to describe it exactly. So I said, "It is the insertion of the male sex organ into the vagina."

Karin hesitated a moment. Then she said thoughtfully: "If this is what is meant, then we have gone all the way."

Then she broke out, "Please do not think that I lied to you yesterday. You are the first one who has told me in a concrete way what is meant. When I had my first period, all my mother said to me was, 'Be careful and don't make anything dirty!'

"That was my whole sex education. Why do they all beat around the bush? 'Don't go all the way! Don't go too far!' But how far too far is, no one ever told me. Is embracing too far? Are kisses too far?"

Karin challenged me. She wanted a precise statement. I thought of many talks which I have had with young people who assured me, sometimes in tears, that they had never intended to go all the way, but then they had been unable to stop.

So I said — and those who know a better answer may correct me —, "The point where it becomes impossible to stop is mostly lying down together and any form of undressing."

It is very hard to make general rules which would fit for everyone everywhere. But this can be a guide: the one who has the more sensitive conscience should be the helper of the other one. A slap on the fingers can be a greater proof of love than a French kiss. The respect for one another will grow and love will deepen. On the other hand, "going all the way" turns out to be a short cut and often means the end of the feeling of love you tried to express.

"Can sex hurt love?"

"Oh, yes, Karin. It certainly can."

A student couple who was expecting a child out of wedlock wrote to me: "Isn't all that matters is that it was done in love?"

I answered: "Love? Love to the baby for whom no proper home is prepared? Love to your partner whose professional career is now messed up? Love to your parents to whom you cause embarrassment and shame? Maybe you solved one problem — you released the sexual tension. But you created many new ones — wedding, home, support, profession . . . love?"

Love is hurt when it is not protected by divine will. Sex can hurt love. Therefore God protects love by confining sex to marriage.

All girls give themselves out of "love" or what they think it is. But not all of them are married by the one to whom they gave themselves. Many a messed-up life started this way. Therefore let me repeat over and over again for those who have such incapable mothers as Karin: even a first and only intercourse can result in pregnancy.

"But," Karin said, "isn't it their own fault if the girl becomes pregnant? When I worried about that, my boy friend calmed my fears by assuring me that he would watch out.

"At first, I did not know what he meant by 'watching out'. Now, I know. He disengaged his member and shed his semen outside my body. But, you see, that way I did not get any satisfaction out of our experience and therefore I thought that we had not gone 'all the way'."

I was glad that Karin had opened up. This method of conception control as she described it provides a sort of satisfaction for the boy but rarely for the girl. This is why this abrupted intercourse — abrupted for the girl — may lay the foundation for a later frigidity or even cause an aversion, a feeling of disgust or loathsomeness in the girl's thinking, towards everything sexual and thus disturb marriage in a decisive way.

So love is hurt **again**.

Besides this fact, the method is also very unesthetic. Neither is it absolutely safe, for the moment of withdrawal can easily be misjudged.

"Is there any absolutely safe means of conception control?" Karin asked.

I don't know of any. Condoms can break. Pessaries can be inaccurately fitted. The so-called "rhythm method", the observation of the infertile days in a woman's menstrual cycle, is certainly not safe, for the periods are not always regular. Especially in premarital situations one can never be sure.

Even with the so-called anti-baby pill, things are not so simple. First of all, the pills have to be prescribed by a medical doctor. But even if one finds a way around that, they are only effective if taken every day between two periods. Missing one day only makes them ineffective. Therefore it is useless to take them along in your purse when going to a dance so that in the case of necessity all you do is swallow a pill quickly beforehand.

Besides that, swallowing a pill daily over a long period of time can have a negative effect on a young girl's organism, for it can change the normal delicate balance of her hormones. As soon as she stops taking them, her ability to conceive may be especially great. Recently cases have become more frequent that more than one egg cell may be released at once. This may result in twin, triplet and even up to octuplet pregnancies. And on the other hand the normal release of egg cells may be inhibited for a long time following cessation of the pills so that the woman is indefinitely sterile. These adverse reactions are not common, but they are absolutely unpredictable and can have tragic consequences.

One girl said: "If I would take pills regularly, calculatingly, in anticipation of a possible sex adventure, I would feel like a prostitute."

"But wouldn't petting then solve all problems?"

When I asked Karin what she meant by petting, she explained that she didn't mean just holding hands or even kissing, but a mutual manipulation of the sex organs until orgasm is reached by both partners, a sort of masturbation together. In this way sexual pleasure can be experienced without fear of pregnancy and still without having to use contraceptives or having to count days.

It may also be easier, because one has not engaged in full intercourse, to calm one's own conscience. I know Christians who believe that they can outwit God in this way. After all, they have not gone "all the way"!

It does look like an ideal solution, but it isn't. It is barking up the wrong tree. It's a dead end road.

Petting used as a method to avoid pregnancy is not absolutely safe either. The percentage of unwanted children produced through petting is surprisingly high. Even the smallest quantity of the male seminal fluid which gets into the vagina is sufficient to fertilize an ovum. It is also true that many couples who start out with petting are unable to stop and then end up in full sexual union in spite of themselves.

But another fact which is widely unknown is still more important.

There are two ways for girls to experience sexual pleasure: a more superficial way which in the final analysis is not satisfactory, and a deep and gratifying way. The latter, however, is normally only a marital possibility for it calls for a harmonious relationship with the same partner over a long period of time. Wives who progress from one way to the other consider the first one as something childish and immature. "For the first time I feel like a real woman!" they say as they experience the deep and gratifying way.

Through petting practices a girl gets used to the superficial way only. Later on in marriage she may have a hard time to mature to the deep and rewarding experience. Thus she makes herself and her husband unhappy.

So love is hurt again. The one who wants sex without marriage will not only be unable to learn love; he will also be unable to protect it. He is not mature and cannot mature.

Years ago a high school student in a talk with me defended petting as something "beautiful". As a college sophomore she wrote to me recently that now she was ashamed of it and felt ill-used. Although she doesn't yet know her future husband, she says she will be ashamed in front of him too because of her past petting experiences.

In this connection, may I briefly point to something else. Many of those who got involved in heavy petting practices and then were left by their partners, slide easily into the habit of masturbation. This is not only true for boys, but for girls as well.

Masturbation is a cry for help. But according to my experience this help must be offered to the individuals in need of it in different ways. May I say this much here: If you are on this wrong track, by no means remain alone, but seek out a trustworthy person and talk over your problem with him.

Karin asked again: "Why didn't someone tell me these things?"

I said: "Karin, I often wonder too what the reason is for this strange silence. Maybe it comes out of a bad conscience. Maybe it comes from a feeling that one lacks authority in a field where one has failed himself. Will you become a better mother for your own children?"

"It's true!" she said, "I had a bad conscience when I said 'yes' to my boy friend. It was painful for my soul. I just pretended to be happy, but I really felt like sobbing and weeping."

"Karin," I said, "if you had only sobbed and wept, he probably would not have gone all the way. You would have challenged him as a man and he would have wanted to protect you. But since you pretended to be happy, he tried to make you happy. That way he injured you."

"I can't understand it," she said, "I did not want it, but he did. But when I gave in, he lost interest. For him it was the end. For me it was a beginning. Can't he understand that?"

"No, Karin, he can't."

"And why?"

"Because he is a boy and you are a girl."

"Well," she said, "it's too late now anyway. What has happened has happened. It can never be undone. My life is all messed up."

"No, Karin," I said, "You're mistaken. For God there is never a too-late. There is no life so messed up, but that He can bring it in order. He is almighty. He can even make done things undone by His forgiveness. For this is what forgiveness means: to make done things undone."

You do not need to continue to live with this pain in your soul. There is a possibility of a new beginning. If you would like to take this step toward a new beginning, may I give you a two-fold advice:

First of all, you will hardly be able to succeed by yourself. You need an experienced spiritual counsellor as a helper.

Secondly, do not stop half way, but make this new beginning a complete one. Here you have a chance to really "go all the way". In cleaning up the mess, don't stop with the sex corner, but clean up the other dark corners as well. Don't confess the transgressions of one commandment only, but bring to the light your transgressions of the other commandments as well.

It may well be that the cause of your failures and defeats in the realm of sex is compromise and disobedience in other areas of life where you disregarded the will of God.

Jesus says: "He who comes to me I will not cast out."

This promise is for you too without reservation. You can accept His offer without fear. With Jesus it pays to go "all the way".